MW01045560

DON'T STOP...
FILL EVERY POT!

THE STORY OF THE WIDOW'S OIL

By Marilyn Lashbrook

Illustrated by Stephanie McFetridge Britt

RAINBOW
STUDIES
INTERNATIONAL

El Reno, Oklahoma

Creating Colorful Treasures™

DON'T STOP...FILL EVERY POT!
will assure your child that God cares
about the daily needs of children.
He or she will learn that when faith
and obedience are present, God shows
His power.

On the second or third reading of the
book, begin to pause each time you
come to one of the small line illustrations
in the text. Wait for your little one
to fill in the word. As your child grows,
let him or her read beginning words
then more and more of the story to you.

Discuss with your child the concept that
partial obedience is disobedience. Talk
about everyday situations in which he or
she has an opportunity to obey fully.

Key:

door

money

sad

house

pots

pot

happy

Library of Congress Catalog Card Number: 93-086766
ISBN 0-933657-75-7

Art direction and design by
Chris Schechner Graphic Design.

1 2 3 4 5 6 7 8 9 — 02 01 00 99
Rainbow Studies International, El Reno, OK 73036, U.S.A.

Don't Stop...
Fill Every Pot!

THE STORY OF THE WIDOW'S OIL

Taken from 2 Kings 4

There was once a woman who had no husband. She had no food. She had no money. But she had plenty of problems.

Knock! Knock! Knock! There was one more problem waiting at the door.

A man was outside. The woman was inside.
She opened the ⬚ .

"Give me the 💵 you owe!" demanded
the man.

"But I have no 💵," the woman said.

"Give me the money, or give me your sons!"
said the man. Then he left.

The woman was very ☹ .

She hurried to find Elisha. Elisha was God's friend.

"My husband owed money to a man," the woman told Elisha, "but now, my husband is dead. I have no money. The man said he will take my sons if I don't pay him."

"How can I help?" asked Elisha. "Tell me what you have in your 🏠."

"Nothing," the woman answered, "except a little oil."

"Go," said Elisha, "Ask all your neighbors for empty pots."

"Don't ask some of your neighbors — ask them all. And don't ask for just a few pots — ask for as many as your friends can lend you."

"Then go inside your 🏠. Shut the 🚪 behind you and your sons. Pour oil into all the ⊖⊖⊖. As each pot is filled, put it aside. Don't stop . . . fill every ⊖!"

The woman had only a tiny bit of oil . . . just a few drips . . . just a few drops. Not enough to fill many pots. Not enough to fill any pots!

But she did not argue. She believed God would do a miracle.

So she and her sons knocked on every
neighbor's  just as Elisha told them. They
borrowed as many  as they could.

There were big pots and small 000. There were short pots and tall 000. Lots and lots of empty pots!

Then they went home and shut the ▢ just as Elisha told them. The woman started pouring her oil into one of the borrowed pots.

The stream of oil kept coming and coming until the pot was full.

Then she filled another ⊖
   and another
      and another.

Her sons moved the full pots and replaced them with empty pots. The more she poured, the more oil there was.

God kept it flowing.

At last, her sons said, "Mom, there are no more empty ⊖⊖⊖ !" Then the oil stopped flowing. Not one more drop.

They looked around the room and wondered
what to do with all that oil.

So the woman went and told Elisha.

"Go sell the oil," Elisha said. "Pay the man what you owe. Then you can use the rest for you and your sons."

First the woman had to sell the oil.

Second, she had to pay what she owed.

Third, she could buy food.

Now the woman was very ☺.
She had food.
She had 💵.
She had her sons.
And best of all, she had a loving
and powerful God.

ME TOO!® BOOKS

Ages 2-7

SOMEONE TO LOVE
THE STORY OF CREATION

TWO BY TWO
THE STORY OF NOAH'S FAITH

I DON'T WANT TO
THE STORY OF JONAH

I MAY BE LITTLE
THE STORY OF DAVID'S GROWTH

I'LL PRAY ANYWAY
THE STORY OF DANIEL

WHO NEEDS A BOAT?
THE STORY OF MOSES

GET LOST, LITTLE BROTHER
THE STORY OF JOSEPH

THE WALL THAT DID NOT FALL
THE STORY OF RAHAB'S FAITH

NO TREE FOR CHRISTMAS
THE STORY OF JESUS' BIRTH

NOW I SEE
THE STORY OF THE MAN BORN BLIND

DON'T ROCK THE BOAT
THE STORY OF THE MIRACULOUS CATCH

OUT ON A LIMB
THE STORY OF ZACCHAEUS

SOWING AND GROWING
THE PARABLE OF THE SOWER AND THE SOILS

DON'T STOP. . . FILL EVERY POT
THE STORY OF THE WIDOW'S OIL

GOOD, BETTER, BEST
THE STORY OF MARY AND MARTHA

GOD'S HAPPY HELPERS
THE STORY OF TABITHA AND FRIENDS

Ages 5-10

IT'S NOT MY FAULT
MAN'S BIG MISTAKE

GOD, PLEASE SEND FIRE
ELIJAH AND THE
PROPHETS OF BAAL

TOO BAD, AHAB
NABOTH'S VINEYARD

THE WEAK STRONGMAN
SAMSON

NOTHING TO FEAR
JESUS WALKS ON WATER

THE BEST DAY EVER
THE STORY OF JESUS

THE GREAT SHAKE-UP
MIRACLES IN PHILIPPI

TWO LADS AND A DAD
THE PRODIGAL SON

NOBODY KNEW BUT GOD
MIRIAM AND BABY MOSES

MORE THAN BEAUTIFUL
THE STORY OF ESTHER

FAITH TO FIGHT
THE STORY OF CALEB

BIG ENEMY, BIGGER GOD
THE STORY OF GIDEON

WE SEE!™ VIDEOS

VIDEOS FOR TODAY'S CHRISTIAN FAMILY.
*51 animated Bible stories from the Old Testament ("In the Beginning" Series) and
New Testament ("A Kingdom without Frontiers" Series) will provide your children
with a solid cornerstone of spiritual support.*

Available at your local bookstore or from:

Rainbow Studies International • P.O. Box 759 • El Reno, Oklahoma 73036

1-800-242-5348

RSI
Creating Colorful Treasures™